AF775897

Copyright © 2026 by Jennifer Breland

All rights reserved. No portion of this book may be reproduced, stored in a retrieval system, or transmitted in any form or by any means—electronic, mechanical, photocopy, recording, or any other—except for brief quotations in printed reviews, without the prior permission of the publisher.

Unless otherwise indicated, Scripture quotations used in this book are taken from the Holy Bible, New International Version®, NIV®. Copyright © 1973, 1978, 1984, 2011 by Biblica, Inc.® Used by permission of Zondervan. All rights reserved worldwide. www.zondervan.com. The "NIV" and "New International Version" are trademarks registered in the United States Patent and Trademark Office by Biblica, Inc.®

Scripture marked nkjv are taken from the New King James Version®. Copyright © 1982 by Thomas Nelson. Used by permission. All rights reserved.

Cover Design: Brad Dennison

Interior Design: Bruce Deroos, Left Coast Design

Printed in the United States of America

PARENTING

Letters and Lessons to

Strengthen Your Family and Faith

Jennifer Breland

Table of Contents

Dedication

To Katie, Lauren, Josh, Jake, and Ryan,
Thank you for teaching me about God's love. I am thankful that I am able to walk this journey of motherhood with you. Your lives continue to encourage me and press me closer to Jesus. You are an inspiration to me every day.

I love you.

To Jeremy, my best friend,
We have encouraged each other, cheered for one another, and prayed that our kids would desire Jesus more than anything. Our prayers have been answered, and I am eternally grateful.

I love you more every day!

Acknowledgments

To Jen Cortez,
Thank you for walking alongside me in this project, it has been an honor. You are wise and such a talented writer and creator. Thank you for being so patient and kind every step of the way. I could not have finished this book without you.

To Dawn Woods,
Your vast experience and consistent drive gave me the confidence to push this book over the finish line. Your consistent drive and persistence caused me to cross the finish line. Your wealth of knowledge gave me confidence that this book was actually going to be completed. Thank you!

To Brad Dennison,
I cannot thank you enough for all of your creative genius. Thank you for being so willing to listen and help me figure out such a beautiful cover for this book.

Mom and Dad,
Thank you for setting the foundation for this book. Your love and encouragement as a child allowed me to dream big, and always depend on God for guidance. I love you.

Introduction

The instant your baby is placed in your arms, the world as you know it changes forever. The love you feel for your newborn is unlike anything you've ever known; it's so strong you can almost reach out and touch it. Yet even while all that love floods your heart, the call of motherhood can also feel overwhelming. Thoughts pour in: *Am I fit for this? Am I going to know what to do when I can't get this little person to stop crying? Do I have enough love to take care of this baby? Will I be enough?*

Mom, you are not alone. In August of 1997, my life turned upside down with the birth of our beautiful daughter, Katie Marie. She brought the most amazing things into our world, and I knew I wanted to be the best mom I could possibly be for her. I remember wondering if I would be enough, too. Then, over the next nine years, God gave us four more unbelievable children, Lauren, Josh, Jake, and Ryan. Each child brought something special to our family, and each one brought a whole new set of things to learn! But with every child and in every circumstance—even the hardest ones—God gave me just what I needed at the exact moment I needed it.

Our children have taught me more lessons than I could ever put into this small book's pages. They have taught me how to find the beauty in the difficult moments, to find new ways of doing ordinary things, and best of all, to see God's love in a thousand new ways.

Life with children, whether you have one or ten, is a life that's bursting at the seams. But I'm here to tell you that *you can be the mother you want to be for your children if you do it in God's strength.* He will be there with you, caring for *you* as you care for your children, filling you up with just what they need as you ask him for grace, wisdom, and insight.

In this little book, I'll share some of the lessons I've learned along the way. It's a book of letters to our children, letters written to them from this luxurious point of view, looking backward, seeing how God was at work in our family and was using us to tell the story of his love.

Whether you have one child or many, whether you have a traditional family structure or one that looks different from mine, you can do this! My prayer is that as you read these pages, you'll feel strengthened and encouraged, knowing God is already telling his story through you.

Love,
Jennifer

Cradled in Prayer

"So do not fear, for I am with you;

do not be dismayed, for I am your God.

I will strengthen you and help you; I will

uphold you with my righteous right hand."

Isaiah 41:10

Dear Lauren,

You were so colicky when you were a newborn that I didn't know if you would *ever stop crying!* It was such a difficult time for us (especially for you)! Dad and I would try to encourage each other, reminding ourselves that newborn crying wouldn't last forever, but we were so immersed in our little world with you, it just felt impossible to believe. To make matters harder, we lived in an apartment back then and shared our little room with you. We were desperate for relief!

We did everything we could to make things better. We discussed my diet and adjusted there. We gave you Mylicon drops for your tummy every day and prayed it would help. We swaddled you tight in my favorite Gymboree blanket and prayed that you would stay asleep just long enough for us to get a couple of hours of rest.

It was my friend Tracy who gave me life-changing advice. She said that when you were quiet and nursing in the early hours of the morning, I should use that time to *pray for you.* She said the sweet, calm times would be rare in those first weeks, and I shouldn't take them for granted. Sure enough, turning those precious quiet moments into times of prayer created a little place of calm for us amid the storm.

You helped us learn patience in those moments, and those hard days strengthened our prayer life in too many ways to count. There were times when I felt ill-equipped to take care of my screaming "bald eagle" (you were bald until the age of two!), but along the way, God reminded me that we were the ones he chose to be your parents, and he would give us the necessary strength to care for you.

I give thanks to God that after a month or so (see, I can't even remember), your colic subsided, and your tears were replaced with the sweetest smiles. Your dad and I may have been upholding you, but God was upholding us all with his righteous right hand. He still is.

I love you,

Mom

In the newborn days, look for quiet moments to spend praying over your child and asking God to strengthen you. He will provide everything you need.

Dear Lord,

Thank you for this precious child. Thank you for knowing exactly what she needs. Please help me to understand her language, and make it clear to me why she is crying. God, you created her inward parts, and I praise you because she is fearfully and wonderfully made. I know, Father, that you made my child especially for me. I trust you today to give me the strength to be able to have peace in the midst of not knowing what to do. I pray that I can love my child with the love that comes directly from you. Help me please. I am weary and need supernatural strength today. I put her in your hands and ask you to calm her. Thank you, Jesus. I believe that you can come into this space right now and calm my spirit and my precious child.

In Jesus's name, Amen.

The Gift of Slowing Down

"Therefore, as God's chosen people, holy and dearly loved, clothe yourselves with compassion, kindness, humility, gentleness and patience."

Colossians 3:12

Dear Josh,

When you came into this world, *my world* began to slow down in the best way. I was used to two girls who were loud and energetic, moving at full speed around the clock. You were going at a different speed than they were, and I'm so glad! You are intentional and thoughtful about everything you do, and I can look back now and see you were always that way. You are exactly who God made you to be.

At first, I wanted to always hurry you along. You would walk when I needed you to run. My focus was scattered as I tried to manage your sisters and daily life, but your steady presence helped me learn to *just sit a little longer.* You would want to talk and process things, and my mind would be worried about dinner or the next appointment. But I loved you so much, and because of that love, I learned to just take a breath and listen. I don't think I would've ever realized how busy my mind always was if you hadn't been there to show me a different way of being. I needed you to slow me down and remind me to take a breath.

When you have shared your heart with me, I've been blown away by your wisdom. I used to tell your teachers to just wait and listen to you when you took extra time to process information, because it would be worth the wait! Your perspective is so deep and insightful.

Thank you for teaching me humility, gentleness, and patience just by being you.

I love you,

Mom

When you have a child with a different temperament and pace than yours, stop and remember this child is a gift, one to be enjoyed and cherished. We often learn the most from those who see things differently from us. Talk to those close to your child (coaches, teachers, and so forth) to explain their temperament; no one knows your child as you do.

Dear Jesus,

Thank you for calling me to be patient, not in my own flesh, but in your Spirit. Thank you for this little one who makes me slow down and listen. Thank you for how this child teaches me about your pace and about how you call us to live differently than the world around us. So many times, I feel impatient and want to solve my problems quickly. Help me to be okay in the waiting. Expand my time and energy, and help me to be still. Father, I know when I process and pray, my words and actions are more thoughtful and helpful. Please help me to be a better listener and not be consumed with having an answer. Teach me to trust you for the answers. God, I know that my timing is not your timing. Help me, Lord, to wait on you.

In Jesus's name, Amen.

In the Dark, God Was Near

"In peace I will lie down and sleep, for you alone, Lord, make me dwell in safety."

Psalm 4:8

Dear Jake and Ryan,

Some things in life are beyond our control, and dealing with your night terrors was one of those things. We felt so scared and confused when you both were experiencing those awful, terrifying dreams.

At first, we tried to reason with you to let you know you were safe, but that never worked! We read everything we could find and tried everything we could think of! We tried taking you to the bathroom or having you pet the dog. You would often tell us what was happening in your dreams and that you were scared. It was like you were with us and not with us all at the same time. We would tell you we needed your help, that we needed you to help us by lying down beside us. Even in the midst of your distress, you would often do what we asked. Eventually, we learned to just hold you tight, turn out the lights, and pray out loud. Usually, after about ten minutes, you would calm down, and the dream would pass.

During the worst nights, we really saw the power of prayer. Once when we started praying, Ryan said, "Yes, help me, Jesus." If we just spoke God's word over you, you would finally fall into a deep sleep. You would never remember what happened, and we were so thankful for that.

The power of prayer is real, and we're so thankful we learned that with you.

I love you,

Mom

When you're in a situation that's outside of your control, the sooner you recognize that, the better. Trying to control those situations only increases anxiety, but turning them over to God through prayer brings peace.

Dear Jesus,

Thank you that you are a God who takes away our fears. Isaiah 41:10 says, "So do not fear, for I am with you; do not be dismayed, for I am your God. I will strengthen you and help you; I will uphold you with my righteous right hand." God, in the middle of these hard nights, help me to picture you holding my child. When I feel out of control, help me to know you are in control. Thank you for giving me guidance and telling me what to do to help my little one. Thank you that your Word is strong and powerful and can eliminate the clutches of the enemy. I pray for our children's safety. I know that you hold each child in the palm of your hand; therefore, they are safe. Your Word says that you will keep in perfect peace those whose minds are set on you (Isaiah 26:3). I entrust my children to you while they sleep tonight.

In Jesus's name, Amen.

The Gift of Sharing a Room

"Let brotherly love continue."

Hebrews 13:1, NKJV

Dear Jake,

I still remember the day you asked me if you could sleep with Josh; you were about six years old. Dad and I hesitated because we thought you both would talk all night and never get to sleep! After giving it some thought, we finally agreed to let you try it. Only a week later, your little brother Ryan begged us to put a mattress on the floor in the room with you and Josh so he could sleep there, too. Your idea was taking on a life of its own! Ryan was only four, and we wondered if you three would *ever* sleep because we didn't think Ryan would ever stop talking! We said yes, though, and now I think that was one of the best decisions we've ever made.

After you all were tucked in at night, sometimes Dad and I would stand outside your door and listen to your conversations. We would laugh at the things you would say, and the stress of our day would just melt away. You would pour your hearts out to each other, talking about difficult situations and things you were dealing with or joking about the funny things that happened that day. You grew to know each other better during those nights. You also learned to be more patient with one another because you found out what was really going on in each other's hearts.

You three always wanted to go to bed early so you could have "more talk time." Sometimes you would bond over the book Dad had read to you, talking about the story you had just heard. We would pray together every night before leaving your room, and the prayers, no matter who said them, were an encouragement to each of us. Thinking back to those nights, I love knowing that in that small, shared room, you and your brothers became so close, and the words you spoke to each other became precious memories.

Sharing a room taught you a lot practically, too. You learned to be clean for your brothers' sake. (You didn't want them to be angry with you!) When Josh was a senior in high school, he told me that he didn't want to move into one of the empty bedrooms because he didn't want to miss a single night with you and Ryan. I'm still amazed at how your relationship grew because of all those talks in the dark. Thank you for choosing to have deep conversations when either of your brothers needed a listening ear.

Your love for your siblings changed their lives, one night at a time, over the course of sixteen years. Thank you for showing us all a new way of letting "brotherly love continue."

I love you,

Mom

Listen to your children's ideas and give weight to them. Actively encourage siblings to connect and spend time together. Those relationships will be some of the most important ones in their lives!

Dear Jesus,

Thank you for allowing me to place my children together in the same room. Thank you for the conversations they will have and the peace they will bring to each other as they talk in the dark. I thank you for being there with them and for directing their words. I pray that where there's dissension, you will bring unity. I pray that you would fill their room with laughter and that they would find joy in one another's company. I pray that they would ask the right questions of one another and have clarity when offering a word of advice. I pray that you would shine a light into their conversation and no evil will be present as they lay in the dark. I pray that when it's time to calm down, they will pray together and sleep peacefully. Thank you for this time apart from the world and all its chaos.

In Jesus's name, Amen.

When Passion Finds Purpose

"Whatever you do, work at it with all your heart, as working for the Lord, not for human masters . . .."

Colossians 3:23

Dear Lauren,
When I think of you, the word that comes to my mind is *passion.*

When you were little, you were obsessed with Gretl from *The Sound of Music* and were determined to grow up to be her. It makes me laugh to think about it now, but even as a tiny girl, you were so passionate! You knew all the way back then that music had something to do with your calling. I can see now that only someone with your intensity could fulfill the call that God has placed on your life. Your independent thinking didn't always align with mine, and that could be hard for both of us. Still, you lived out of a place of depth and devotion. You showed love and care for others' needs and such a deep love for music.

It took a little while for your natural intensity to find its proper channel. When we were homeschooling, you could hardly focus for more than a couple of minutes. Your attention span was so small! I remember asking you to "please write important things on your hand" or "make a note of what you need to remember." But as an adult, it seems you can overcome any obstacle or solve any problem that stands in your way; you're so focused and driven. I marvel at God's goodness when I see the woman you have become.

You helped me understand why God says, repeatedly, not to judge one another but to bear with one another in love. We are all changing and growing, aren't we?

You are a difference-maker, a visionary, and an influencer with incredible leadership qualities. I couldn't be prouder of the woman you are becoming. I hope I'm still becoming a woman who makes you proud, too.

I love you,

Mom

When your child shows "difficult behavior" and strong independent thinking, practice seeing it as passion and strength. Children test us because they feel secure with us and know we will love them no matter what. We are a safe place for them to figure out where the line is. Ask God to direct that strength into a powerful force for good in the world!

Dear Jesus,

Thank you for our children who push our buttons and cause us to need you more! I pray in the hard moments that you would strengthen me to remember that my child is changing day after day. In those moments when I live in the flesh and want to judge the way she's behaving, help me to remember that you are the only one who truly knows her heart. I trust that you are changing her day by day from the inside out. There are so many things I don't understand about who she is at this stage of her life, but you are her creator, and you know her better than I ever could. I long to know her and to be the best mom I can, so please, God, help me in the moments when I just don't understand. Help me to listen with your ears. Help me to see what you see and to love her despite what I feel. I claim in Jesus's name that she will begin to understand the magnitude of my love and, most importantly, yours, Lord. I pray you would give me strength to speak with patience as I train my child to practice the way of you.

In Jesus's name, Amen.

Persevering Through Tough Friendships

"Dear friends, let us love one another, for love comes from God. Everyone who loves has been born of God and knows God."

1 John 4:7

Dear Katie,

I remember a time when you were trying to be a good friend to a young lady who was not easy to be around. You invited her to get coffee to try to encourage her, but she spoke so negatively about everything. It was hard to reach her. I know you had a hard time spending time with that friend, but your kindness made an impact on her. She told you that you were just like sunshine and said, "Who wouldn't want to be around the sun?" She said she wasn't like that, and that often people didn't take the time to get to know her. It was a beautiful compliment to you, but also a sad thing to say about herself.

I challenged you that day to continue reaching out to her just twenty seconds at a time. We humans are messy and hard, but we all need encouragement. When we're having a conversation with one of these more challenging friends, we can ask God to help us see the good in them and to understand why they are the way they are. We can pray that he'll give us eyes to see them as *he* sees them. We can ask, "What troubles or difficulties have they faced in their own lives that have made it harder for them to be a good friend?" These are some of the ways God's Spirit makes us more loving and more like Jesus.

Your joy is contagious because it isn't rooted in temporary things but in the eternal love of Christ, which never changes. You are a light to everyone you meet. I see the light of Jesus in you, and I'm so thankful for how it shines in our family and the world. Thank you for being such a good friend to others (and to me).

I love you,
Mom

Help your child learn how to be a good friend by looking for small ways to love those who might be challenging. It doesn't take much time to make a major impact on someone's life. Pray with your child and ask God to help you both see others as he sees them and to love others as he does.

Dear Lord,

I pray for my child's friends. I pray that you would help them understand each other and love each other more every time they are together. I pray that they would communicate clearly and encourage each other. My child desires deep friendships, so please give her wisdom to be able to discern what her friends need from her. I pray that, in the difficult conversations, she and her friends will show understanding and an openness to hear one another's opinions. At the same time, I pray that my child will be bold and never feel pressured to do something that goes against her convictions. For that friend who is unlovely, help my child love her out of the abundance of your love. Help me to give wise counsel when instructing my child on how to be a good friend. I pray my heart would never judge a friend by past actions but would trust that you are working in his or her life and heart. I need you, Lord, because I know every child is different and is growing at his or her own pace.

In Jesus's name, Amen.

Wisdom That Listens

"My [child], if your heart is wise,

then my heart will be glad indeed;

my inmost being will rejoice when

your lips speak what is right."

Proverbs 23:15-16

Dear Ryan,

Thank you for reminding me to be quick to listen, even if I feel like I already have an answer. You are a gifted communicator, and I've been humbled when you've asked me to just stop talking and *listen*. Sometimes I need to remember that listening is as much a part of communicating as speaking. You are wise beyond your years. I pray that you lean into the wisdom of God so that your gift of persuasion will always serve his kingdom and his purposes, because people listen when you speak!

Others want to follow your lead because you genuinely care about them; your sensitive spirit is so evident. This sensitivity is one of your greatest gifts. Seek the Lord with all your heart, and you will influence more people than you can imagine. As he fills more and more of you with his Spirit, your wisdom will continue to increase. Questions may fill your mind as you wrestle with life, and it will be easy to lean on your understanding, but if you remember to ask God to give you the answers, he will! He is working in and through you every day. I hope that I have told you often enough about all the good that I see in you.

I love you,

Mom

Listening to your child is just as important as speaking to him or her. Practice slowing down and remembering to listen—to your child and to the Lord.

Dear Lord,

Help me to be a better listener. As my child processes his or her thoughts, may I wait patiently and listen with the awareness that the first words they say may not really be what they mean. I want to be a better listener. I pray as it says in James 1:19 that I would be slow to speak, quick to listen, and slow to become angry. It's very easy, Lord, for me to think that I should have an answer for every question my child asks me. Help me to be content to pause. May I have the discernment to know if I should stop and pray with my child in the middle of a conversation. Please help me not to react or jump to conclusions and get overwhelmed by their words. Help me to pray continually for future conversations so that when they come, I will be ready. Thank you for promising to be with me in the difficult journey of parenting.

In Jesus's name, Amen.

One Act of Service
Can Change Everything

"And do not forget to do good and to share with others, for with such sacrifices God is pleased."

Hebrews 13:16

Dear Josh,

Thank you for having such a compassionate heart. The week of your tenth birthday, I asked you what you wanted to do for your special day. I could never have dreamed of what you would say! You looked me right in the eye and said with conviction, "Mom, I want to go and serve the homeless community." I was blown away. I couldn't believe that *this* was how you wanted to spend *your birthday!*

I'll admit, I was nervous about taking you and your brothers and sisters into the heart of Nashville at night. I thought about the dangerous situations that could arise and wondered how Dad and I could keep five children safe, but I wanted to follow your lead and honor the godly desire stirring in your heart. We found a ministry called "People Loving Nashville," and we volunteered to serve alongside them on the evening of your tenth birthday. That night changed the trajectory of our lives, Josh.

As you shared your heart with the other volunteers and the ministry founders, something beautiful happened; a new passion began to rise in *their* hearts. I remember our family and the team leaders just crying as we sat in the parking lot of that old church in Nashville. The ministry founders had grown weary in the face of such relentless, enormous work, and the presence of a boy like you wanting to help gave *them* fresh energy to keep going.

Serving as a family helped us all become a little more grateful and a little less selfish. Now your brother will never let me pass an unhoused person without helping them in some way. He has a new awareness of these vulnerable members of our community. Remember the five-dollar McDonald's gift cards we've bought and passed out over the years? And remember the man selling the newspapers? We had a small conversation with him, hoping he would feel loved and important, too. Your bravery that night had a ripple effect on us and so many others.

For two years, we spent most Monday nights serving those in our local community because of you and your sensitive heart. Thank you, Josh, for being humble, unselfish, and courageous. You've taught me a new way to "serve one another humbly in love" (Galatians 5:13).

I love you,

Mom

When your child wants to do something good that makes you feel afraid, pause and pray. Don't say no right away. When we step out of our comfort zone and serve others without knowing what may happen, we all see the faithfulness of God unfold before our eyes.

Dear Lord,

I pray that my children will desire to serve you and to serve others. When my child asks to reach out to another person, may I always say yes. You, Lord, know the deep needs of your people; I ask you for discernment to know when I should step in and help another family, whether we have a relationship with them or not. I don't want to miss your voice just because I am comfortable. Show me and each member of our family your plan for us in serving our community and those around the world. Thank you for being the perfect example of servanthood. Thank you for reminding me in your Word that "a little child will lead them" (Isaiah 11:6). I pray that we would walk alongside each other as we serve, and that it would deepen our relationships. I pray that as we serve, people will see your light. May they always recognize that every good and perfect gift is from you, Lord. Thank you for the opportunity to serve one another.

In Jesus's name, Amen.

When Hard Questions Lead to Understanding

"[D]o not worry about what to say or how to say it. At that time you will be given what to say, for it will not be you speaking, but the Spirit of your Father speaking through you."

Matthew 10:19b-20

Dear Ryan,

Thank you for asking me hard questions, the kind of questions that often scare me. Remember that night in the 6th grade when you asked me why we should even want to have a relationship with God? That question made a deep impression on me, and it helped me grow in my own relationship with God. While trying to answer your question in my own mind, I realized that my very being longs for a relationship with him. We're all made in his likeness, and we have a void that can only be filled by his Spirit. It's impossible to be complete and have true joy and peace without God. Reflecting on this question brought me to new levels of understanding in my own spirit. Thank you, Ryan, for opening my mind that night and for really challenging me.

I often fear that I won't know what to say when you ask me hard questions, but being your mom has taught me to trust in God's moment-by-moment faithfulness. I'm always amazed at how he gives me the wisdom I need to communicate with you right when I need it! I don't parent perfectly, but I'm learning as we go, too.

Remember that day when we were talking about rules in our house that you just didn't understand? At first, I felt frustrated because we had talked about those rules so many times. I thought I had made it crystal clear why those rules were in place, but you didn't understand the why beneath the rule. I remember you saying you "just wanted to understand." I can see now that you were thinking more deeply and just needed a deeper answer. At that moment, I decided to empathize with you and to come alongside you instead of trying to tower over you. I began talking about how certain rules in life really bothered me, too. That mental shift helped diffuse the anger between us, because we found a little piece of common ground to stand on together. Suddenly, we were confiding in each other instead of opposing each other. God gave me the wisdom I needed!

I understand now that it's important to stay open to your questions, because even though we may have rehashed the same thing repeatedly, I still need to listen when you're working through something. I may not change my mind on the issue, but we can at least work to *understand each other* when we're grappling with something. We can find common ground *somewhere.*

I really love you, and I want to be more patient. Thank you for being patient with me.

I love you,
Mom

In the push-and-pull of difficult parenting moments, stop and ask God to help you connect with your child; he will faithfully show you how. Actively listening makes your child feel understood, builds trust, and establishes a deeper connection between you.

Dear Lord,

Thank you for understanding my child perfectly. When I can't figure out the words to say, make your plan clear to me. I pray that in each situation you would strengthen me and give me the boldness to speak with authority from your Word. I pray that I would speak with grace and understand that my child doesn't know what he doesn't know, and that life's experience will bring him more wisdom as he grows. I want to give our child the best advice I can. Help me to be patient with myself as I grow in you and begin to understand more of what my child needs. When I don't know what to say, help me to pause and pray. If I feel like I need more time, help me to tell my child I need to pray before I give an answer. Thank you, God, that you promise to help me. Thank you that when I don't know what to say, and I tell my child I need to pray, it points to the fact that I need your wisdom, Lord. Let me model what it looks like for my child to take all of his concerns to you.

In Jesus's name, Amen.

Speaking the Truth with Boldness

"Guide me in your truth and teach me,

for you are God my Savior, and my

hope is in you all day long."

Psalm 25:5

Dear Ryan,

The way you communicate is so refreshing. Many people are afraid to say things that go against the grain of their social environments because they don't want to make waves or ruffle feathers. You're not that way. You've always had such an authentic and truthful spirit, and your words align with who you are and what you really believe. I appreciate that about you.

Your boldness has been an encouragement in our family, too. We all have different strengths and challenges, and I remember a time when you were talking to Jake and encouraging him not to be afraid of new situations. You said, "Jake, you have the drive and motivation to do anything. You are naturally talented and so good at everything you do!" Then you told Jake that you were very comfortable in new situations; you would try anything. You said you needed to pray for more drive and motivation, and he needed to pray to be more confident to try new things. I loved hearing you reflect on how you both needed Jesus.

"I can be lazy," you admitted. "I've been praying about having more motivation and discipline, but the Lord hasn't answered that prayer, yet." You were one hundred percent serious, and I laughed so hard!

Thank you for being honest and saying things we need to hear. Stay true to who God has made you to be and remember that He will continue to use you in a mighty way. So often, God was speaking to us through you!

I love you,

Mom

A child's boldness and directness are often a leadership gift. Instead of taking boldness as a personal attack, try to lean in, listen, and understand. Teach them to express their thoughts respectfully, but value them. These children are world changers!

Dear Lord,

Thank you for our children who are bold. Oftentimes, my patience wears thin, and I need you. I pray that I will be unoffendable as I communicate with my bold children. Help me in the moment to pray under my breath. I pray that I will remember that I am the grown-up, and you will give me the power and wisdom to speak with authority as the parent. Help me to be patient, and help me to repeat what I firmly believe, even though my child may continue to argue his or her point. I want to be firm but also fair, loving, and understanding in the hard conversations. Thank you for the strength of my children's boldness, and may you use it to further your kingdom.

In Jesus's name, Amen.

Learning to Listen Together

"Therefore, my brothers and sisters, you whom I love and long for, my joy and crown, stand firm in the Lord in this way, dear friends!"

Philippians 4:1

Dear Lauren,

I know that many times when you were growing up, you didn't feel like I was listening to you. You felt like you always needed to state your case and prove your point, and at the time, it just felt like you were arguing with everything Dad and I spoke!

As an adult, you've told me you used to think that if I could just *understand you*, I would see things your way and change my mind. That's why you wouldn't back down. You wanted me to understand what you were trying to say. I may have thought you were being stubborn then, but now I see you were just trying to communicate with me! Parenting can be so hard because *it can be so hard to understand each other*. Still, I was holding boundaries that I knew were for your good and your safety. God helped me stand firm with you, and if he hadn't, I'm sure I would've caved many times!

As you matured, God showed you that you didn't always have to state all your reasons or be *right*. That insight brought so much peace to our relationship, and it probably allowed me to relax a little more and understand you better.

I prayed for you so often during those times. I prayed for wisdom and for God to help you listen and learn. I think he taught me to listen and learn just as much as he taught you. God was working in both of us all along.

I love you,

Mom

When you have a child who often stands in opposition to you, lean on Christ and stand firm in him. He will help you hold your ground. And be encouraged! This child will teach you how to persevere in prayer, and God will use those prayers to bear fruit in that child's life.

Dear Lord,

I need your wisdom right now! I am feeling overwhelmed by the magnitude of my child. My child's personality is huge, and her passion in life is causing me a lot of frustration! Lord, I want to be helpful and to never hurt her spirit, but sometimes the conversations are overwhelming, and I lack peace. Please Lord, fill me with direction. Thank you, Lord, for creating my children and for helping me guide them in every season of their lives. Thank you, Lord, that I was created to be their mother. I don't know the outcome of the situation, but I trust you. I feel like I should know what path they need to go down, but so many times, I'm uncertain. Help me to always come to you. I know you are faithful, Lord. Help us both to grow and understand your faithfulness. I commit myself and my child to you.

In Jesus's name, Amen.

Made to Change the World

"My [child], if your heart is wise,

then my heart will be glad indeed;

my inmost being will rejoice when

your lips speak what is right."

Proverbs 23:15-16

Dear Lauren,

I am so happy that God filled you with a strong and powerful spirit. I must admit that when you were younger, I wondered some days whether I would be able to keep it together! You were so strong-minded!

I spent so much time praying for you. On the hard days, I would sometimes go into my room and cry, wondering how I would ever get you to understand that I loved you and just wanted the best for you. Looking back now, I see how close I grew to the Lord through those prayers. He was teaching me to entrust you to him. And one day there came a moment when God opened my eyes to the truth that your passion—your *strength of spirit*—was the very thing that was going to change this world. The Lord showed me in my spirit that he had made you in such a way that if you believed strongly in something, *nothing* and *no one* could change your mind.

We had many difficult conversations, didn't we? Now I'm so thankful for every single one of them, because those conversations allowed me to see your heart. And though some days I wondered if it would ever happen, God did eventually soften that beautiful heart of yours. He answered our prayers for you.

I still remember the day I started seeing that change happening. We were in the car, and you said, "I realized today that there are some battles I just can't fight; I must let certain things go. I need to just say, 'Okay, I understand'—even if I don't—because you and Dad usually know what's best. I guess I will eventually understand."

I almost wrecked the car!

I remember you telling me many things you were learning and discovering in high school; I would laugh inside because they were the very things I had tried to tell you for years! Even with all my striving and effort, I couldn't force you to believe my words; you needed to learn these lessons in your own way.

This new insight into your passionate heart helped shape my prayers for you. I began to pray that you would understand how much God loves the world and how lost people are without him. I knew if you became passionate about people and their need for a Savior, you would indeed change the world. And look at you now—my little firecracker serving the church in full-time ministry! Now you're not determined to prove your point; you're determined to show others the love of God and how their life is incomplete without him. Look at what God has done through you. I'm so proud of you, Lauren.

I love you,

Mom

While rewards and consequences can help teach appropriate behavior, it takes patience and conversations to connect at the heart. Continue to pray for your children and trust God to finish the good work he has started in them.

Dear Lord,

Thank you for my child who speaks with great conviction. I pray that I would stop long enough to hear her and to understand her perspective. I pray that you'll help me sort out what she is actually trying to say. Lord, help me to ask good questions along the way. When I am in a conversation, I often have so many things to say; help me know when to be quiet. I want to give good advice and be loving, but sometimes I make mistakes and need your help. While she is speaking, please help me to listen with intentionality and not be thinking about what I am going to say next. Help me Lord, not to interrupt her. When I speak in anger, I pray that I would be quick to apologize, move past my inadequacies, and put my trust in you. Help me to forgive myself when I fail, and allow it to cause me to press deeper into you. May I pray without ceasing every day for wisdom from you.

In Jesus's name, Amen.

Carrying More Than You Know

"Be completely humble and gentle;

be patient, bearing with one another in love."

Ephesians 4:2

Dear Katie,

You are the oldest child, and with that role comes great responsibility. The oldest sibling always carries a burden that the younger siblings don't quite understand. You must share your things and your time. You must help more and adapt to each new child that joins the family. Your parents rely on you more than they rely on your siblings. I know it's a lot to carry, and I want you to know that I see you and appreciate you.

Sometimes it may feel overwhelming to be the oldest, but God himself gave you this position in our family; you were the one he wanted to come first. *Remember that a willing heart always proves successful.* Walk each day with the knowledge that you are enough, and God will give you the words to share with your siblings. Sometimes you don't feel like you have all the answers, but it's okay. You can be confident that God will be faithful to you. Whether it's being the first to leave for kindergarten, navigating middle school, leaving for college, every experience will serve as a testimony to God's faithfulness. Your struggles will be an example that will help your siblings succeed, so no hard thing you walk through will ever be wasted.

Never underestimate your ability to influence your siblings; they are watching to see how you will point them to God or how you relate to Dad and me in everyday situations.

The joy you bring every time you come home ripples through the family from the moment you walk through the door. I hope we can continue to be an encouragement and support to you. You are a joy to our hearts.

I love you,

Mom

The oldest child needs and deserves lots of encouragement and support. Take time to tell your oldest child how much you appreciate him or her and find ways to do special things just for that child.

Dear Lord,

Thank you so much for our firstborn children. Thank you for equipping them in a special way. I trust, Lord, that you will help them navigate their role in our family. When they feel overwhelmed, I pray that we would encourage them and let them know often how proud we are of their patience with their younger siblings. I pray that they would give their siblings grace and understand how to encourage them. I know their brothers and sisters are watching their every move, and I pray that they would understand the magnitude of their role in the family. In that, though, I pray that they would have complete confidence in the ability you have given them to have a godly impact. Lord, help me know when to give them a break and give me wisdom to understand their individual needs. I pray they will be strong leaders and that they will understand that you are with them every step of the way. Thank you for our firstborn children, and may they desire you more than anything in this life.

In Jesus's name, Amen.

Encouragement Matters

"May the God who gives endurance and encouragement give you the same attitude of mind toward each other that Christ Jesus had, so that with one mind and one voice you may glorify the God and Father of our Lord Jesus Christ."

Romans 15:5-6

Dear Lauren,

I think it's really hard sometimes for adults to remember what it was like to be a kid. I'm sure it can seem like all parents do is point out what our children need to do better or differently. But now that you're an adult, you've told me that when Dad or I pointed out something you were doing *well,* it meant the world to you.

For example, if we told you to study more or to encourage your siblings more, we would watch to see how you were doing. So often we'd see you doing the very things we'd asked you to do! You said our encouragement helped because it showed you that your own efforts were paying off. You'd think, *Oh! I guess I am getting better at that!*

Life can be really tough, and the changes we strive for come in really small steps. Sometimes that change can be so gradual that we don't even see it, and we can be tempted to give up and stop trying. We all long to be seen, and we all need encouragement. Thank you for teaching me that.

I love you,

Mom

It's so important to see your child's efforts and point them out when you see that child making progress. Sometimes all our children hear are our corrections and criticisms, but our encouragement can make an even bigger impact!

Dear Lord,

Help me to not only notice the large accomplishments my children make, but, more importantly, help me see the small accomplishments they make each day. Help me point out these little wins and encourage them to keep moving forward. Lord, help me to remind them that this life is more like playing chess than checkers. We know you are working behind the scenes, and even if we don't see the many things you are accomplishing this day, we believe that you are working all things together for our good. When my child's ugly side comes out, help me to be an example of your beauty. When I don't have the words to say, help me to speak the name *Jesus* and trust you. I know my child is growing and maturing, and when I'm too blinded by baggage in my own life, please allow me to see clearly what you see for our child. Today, no matter what I see, I trust that you are faithful. I am confident that you who began a good work in my child "will carry it on to completion until the day of Christ Jesus" (Philippians 1:6).

In Jesus's name, Amen.

When I Learned to Listen

"Wisdom's instruction is to fear the LORD,

and humility comes before honor."

Proverbs 15:33

Dear Ryan,

You often internalized your hardships and carried your burdens quietly. Sometimes you acted like you were fine and didn't need anything, but the truth was, you *weren't* fine. During those days, I could sense you needed support, but I didn't know how to give it in the way you needed it. I learned to ask God to give me questions to help you open up. I would ask you, "What's your opinion on what we're doing here?" or "What do you think about what's going on with your sibling?"

If I asked you questions directly, it gave you permission to open up and share what was really going on with *you.* I think it helped you grow in confidence and find your voice, too. I may have started asking you questions in order to help you, but in the end, I think your answers helped me just as much.

Your feelings matter so much to me. *You* matter so much. Your humility is so beautiful, and your wisdom runs deep. Because of you, I've learned new ways to fear the Lord and to grow in humility, too. It seems like connecting with her child should be easy for a mom, but it wasn't always easy. And yet, God faithfully provided a way forward for us both.

I love you,

Mom

When you have a child who is more reserved and has a hard time sharing struggles with you, ask God for specific questions to ask that child. Keep a note of the questions and the answers, and you'll be amazed to look back and see how much you've both grown.

Dear Lord,

My child is often so quiet about what is going on in his life. I struggle to identify what he really needs, and I need your guidance. Lord, help me to trust that you will give me the wisdom I need to parent this child. I know that you have given me this child, and I was made to be his mom, but sometimes I live in fear. I fear that I may miss something my child needs. Father, help me to understand that you are the one who has the answers to all the questions that play in my child's head each day. Please, Lord, give me the questions to ask so I can point him to you. I pray that the Word of God would be the loudest words in his mind as he grows up. I pray the noise of this world would not fill his head with lies, but the truth of your Word would fill his soul with a deep understanding that he is your child. I pray that he would understand his worth lies in who you created him to be. I believe my child is growing, and you will provide a way for us to communicate in a powerful and effective way.

In Jesus's name, Amen.

The Power of Birth Order

"Don't let anyone look down on you because you are young, but set an example for the believers in speech, in conduct, in love, in faith and in purity."

1 Timothy 4:12

Dear Josh,

Thank you for leading and loving your brothers so well. All your life, you've had a great love and sensitivity for Jake and Ryan. God gave you the wisdom from a very young age to encourage and include them. I know it was probably annoying when they would copy your every move, but I think you came to understand that they just wanted to be like their big brother.

I'm sure it was hard to always have to share your toys and your things, but you did it without complaining. You showed your brothers the love of Christ with such a generous spirit. You always included them when you had a friend over (even though they were younger and sometimes immature), and I know they felt loved and valued by you. You instilled confidence in them just by letting them be a part of your world.

I think the way you are silly and carefree with your brothers has helped them learn how to live in the moment. It's extraordinary that you can be *so responsible* and *so fun* at the same time.

From the time you were tiny, we would pray over you and your siblings, "God give you wisdom, wisdom beyond your years." You *are* wise beyond your years, Josh. Your influence continues to be profound in your siblings' lives and in ours.

I love you,

Mom

It's important to encourage and empower the oldest brother to help shepherd and lead the younger ones. Remind your kids that God put them in a certain birth order because he trusted them and the influence they would have on their younger siblings.

Dear Jesus,

Help me to trust you in the coming days. As my child begins to understand who he is in Christ, I pray you would pour your wisdom into his heart. I pray that he would seek you each morning and that your words would come alive. As he reads the Bible, I ask that he have the confidence to know that he can lead his siblings well—not in his own strength but in yours. When he feels inadequate, I pray Lord that one of his siblings would encourage him and tell him how thankful they are to have him as their brother. God, you have great plans for my child, and I trust you. I don't trust any more in what I see, but I trust what I know about your word that promises you will never leave my child nor forsake him. Thank you that he is yours. I place him in your hands to do the job that you have created him to do. Thank you for the leader my child is and for what you will do in his heart in the coming days. Help him to never tire of doing what is right.

In Jesus's name, Amen.

Strength That Inspires

"For the eyes of the Lord range throughout the earth to strengthen those whose hearts are fully committed to him."

2 Chronicles 16:9a

Dear Jake,

I hope you know how much of an inspiration you are to me. You have this amazing combination of drive and sensitivity that makes it seem like you can do absolutely anything! Don't ever let your fear of failure cause you to stop reaching beyond what you may think is possible. I really do believe you can do anything! I know all my requests and interruptions must have been difficult at times, but without hesitation, you always stopped what you were doing and helped me. Thank you so much for that.

I've been reflecting on why you can work with such excellence, and I think it's because your work flows out of who you are, out of your inner character and your commitment to God. I see how he strengthens you and supports you. I'm glad he does, because I've often wondered if I give you enough encouragement to vent your frustrations and concerns. I pray as you grow into adulthood, you'll be true to how you feel, with the understanding that I will always love you no matter what.

You are important to me, and I value you more than I can possibly say. Thank you for being such an example of faithfulness and strength to us all.

I love you,

Mom

When children are responsible, driven, and quiet, it's important to ask them good questions and check in with them regularly. It's easy to overlook them. You can set a calendar reminder to check in or plan a special date every few weeks to let them know how much you value them.

Dear Lord,

I thank you for my child who desires to do the right thing and work with all his might. I pray that his accomplishments would not be the source of his happiness or his feelings of worthiness. I pray that what you did on the cross for him would cause him to have confidence that is unwavering. I pray that he will be brave enough to do hard things. When he is unsure of his ability, I pray that he would press into Ephesians 3:20, knowing that you are able to do immeasurably more than we could ever ask or imagine. Please help him not to rely on his own flesh but on your Spirit working in and through him to accomplish what you have set out for him to do. I pray that he would trust that with you, all things are possible (Matthew 19:26). When my child feels like he's carrying the weight of the world, I pray that he will know you are able to lighten his load and give him the energy he needs in all things. Thank you, Father, that you are the God of the impossible and that even though he may be fearful, you will give him courage to press into any obstacle that comes his way.

In Jesus's name, Amen.

Using Our Platform for God

"He holds success in store for the upright, he is a shield to those whose walk is blameless, for he guards the course of the just and protects the way of his faithful ones."

Proverbs 2:7–8

Dear Katie,

I still remember a conversation you and I had in the car during one of your college breaks. You shared how any success we achieve can help us create a platform to share God's glory with others.

You said that when we achieve high levels of success in a sport, the arts, or academics, we begin to look different from the rest of the world. People start to notice our success and give our words more weight. We talked about the boys, their sports, and what might happen if God granted them the success they were working toward. If they found themselves being interviewed and asked how they accomplished so much, they could shine the spotlight on Jesus. You said that any platform we have is an opportunity to lift up God's name and share about his love for us.

Katie, it reminded me of the time Clemson beat Alabama! Clemson's football coach gave all the credit to the Lord. He didn't hide his faith; he told the world about who God is and why he is so joyful. He didn't use his platform to elevate Clemson football; he used it to elevate the name of Jesus. (I know it's tempting to like Clemson now, but remember: Roll Tide!)

The things we believe in become contagious when we share them passionately. The ways of the Lord are right and true; he is perfect in all his ways. He will do whatever is necessary to bring people to himself. His love is just that great!

Using Our Platform for God

Thanks to you, Katie, our family dreams together about how God will use our lives and our accomplishments to influence others for Him. You reminded us to put Jesus on a platform and not ourselves. Thank you for pointing us back to Christ.

I love you,

Mom

Encourage your children to connect their success to God's glory. Teach them that their abilities and gifts come from him, and that they can use those gifts to share the love of Jesus with others!

Dear Lord,

We pray that our children's lives point to you. Whatever is accomplished through our children, may you receive all the glory! When they feel proud, may they remember it is because of you that they are able to fulfill the dreams or visions you have put in their hearts. I pray that you would help them to desire your will for their lives. I pray that their influence would count for kingdom building. When they feel the desire to fulfill their earthly lives with the things of this world, I pray you would bring them back to yourself through other believers and your Word. Help them to understand that nothing is impossible with you. I pray that the people around them would desire the light that is shining in them. We love you and honor you.

In Jesus's name, Amen.

From My Hands to His

"Commit your way to the Lord;

trust in him and he will do this."

Psalm 37:5

Dear Katie,

When you left for college, I thought I was going to die of sadness! I know that sounds dramatic, but I missed you so, so much. It was hard to walk into our kitchen and not have you there to help me or to catch up on all the personal things going on in our lives. I missed your smile, your company—your friendship! Sometimes I would walk into your room and wonder if I had spent enough time just sitting on your bed, talking with you over the years. Where did all the time go?

One morning, I was exercising and telling God how much I missed you and how worried I was about your safety. You were all on your own in a new place. And would your faith hold strong in this new environment? I was afraid of so many things. I felt God say to me in that moment, *Don't you know that I love her so much more than you ever could?* I knew right then that he would protect you. I knew deep in my soul that I didn't have to worry.

I had already seen your unshakeable foundation of faith, and I had to just have faith that I had done my job as a mom. Your Dad and I had prayed for you to have wisdom from the day you were born; now we had to trust you to use it. Sure enough, I watched you grow into a leader as you were challenged in your faith during that first year of college. You pressed into those challenges and learned from them, and God was with you every step of the way. I am so proud of you, Katie.

Thank you for teaching me how to let go and let you be you.

I love you,

Mom

You can trust God to love your child more than you ever could. He will bless your parenting efforts, and he will keep your child close to his heart always. You can rest in his faithfulness.

Dear Jesus,

I love my child so much, and today I am having trouble being separated from her. I miss seeing her face every day, and I miss seeing her come down the stairs from her room each morning. I know you love her more than I ever could, so help me trust you to take care of her when I'm not with her. She is yours, and I commit her back to you. Thank you for loving her more than I ever could. I know that you will use her to influence her new community for the kingdom of God. Help her to withstand the temptations of this world and walk with confidence in the light of who you are. Thank you for giving me these last eighteen years to set a firm foundation with your help. May my child choose to pursue you even when I am not there to encourage her. May she pray and trust that you are with her wherever she goes.

In Jesus's name, Amen.

Strength Through Struggle

"Cast all your anxiety on him

because he cares for you."

1 Peter 5:7

Dear Jake,

Soccer has always been your place to shine, and watching you on the soccer field has brought so much joy to our family. But I also remember a time when that same field became a place of pain for you. All that hard work took a toll on your body, and when you found yourself sidelined with an injury, it rattled you. Do you remember?

What moves me most, looking back, is how you were praying about everything you were going through. You told me that God had been using this struggle to show you that your soccer game wasn't all about you. You said you were there, not only to play, but to encourage your team members and to strengthen the team as a whole.

You saw that God wasn't abandoning you in your injuries; he was teaching you through them. And God showed up for you in miraculous ways. Remember how quickly your shoulder healed? The doctors were awestruck!

Through the anxiety and pain of those injuries, you saw God working in deeper ways in your life. And look at how he met you there in those painful days and brought something beautiful from it. I'm so glad you shared your heart with me, Jake. It was amazing that, through all the injuries, you discovered physical therapy and realized you wanted to help others through medicine. In your struggle, you found a calling. You gave your anxiety to God, and he cared for you, just like he promised he would.

I love you,
Mom

Teach your children to pray little prayers all throughout their childhood. When something is hard or scary, take a moment to stop and pray with your child. These simple acts of faith teach your children how to turn to God, so that when they're older, this will be a well-worn path for them to follow.

Jesus,

I long for my children to understand that their difficulties produce perseverance, and that perseverance must finish its work so they may be mature and complete, not lacking for anything (James 1:4). God, it is so hard to see our children hurt. Help me to recognize that you are their rescuer, and that sometimes I need to be quiet in order for you to work. Help me to never feel guilty when I feel your prompting to be still. Lord, I trust that the seasons they go through will produce a strength in them that I can't understand right now. In these difficult moments, may my children recognize the goodness of a loving Father. May they see your faithfulness in all of life's situations. Please help them recall the little ways you've encouraged them and have sent others to encourage them in difficult seasons. I trust you, Lord, with my children. Please help me to never forget that they are yours.

In Jesus's name, Amen.

Grace in the Transition

"Jesus Christ is the same yesterday and today and forever."

Hebrews 13:8

Dear Katie,

Today I was thinking about the first time you had a break during your freshman year of college. You were constantly on your phone, talking to your friends. You were trying to stay connected with them, but that meant you weren't very connected to us. Remember the talk Dad and I had with you at the coffee shop in Mobile? That was such a hard conversation! We told you how you were home in body only, and we didn't want to waste our short time together. As we talked and cried, we all realized it was a hard thing to be independent for a couple of months and then come back into a supervised environment again where your parents and siblings wanted so much of your attention. I was having some trouble with my own emotions because *I really missed you.* Your everyday life had changed and was so exciting, but for us, life was the same as ever, only with a big hole where you used to be!

I remember you listening to us that day with such tenderness and receptivity. Thank you for sharing your side and for hearing ours, too.

It took a little adjusting, but your college days turned out to be wonderful for all of us. We were so proud of the way you handled your independence. You called us and checked in with your big family often, and you extended so much grace to your dad and me while we learned how to have an adult child. (And we were much better at parenting college kids by the time your sister and brothers left for college!)

Together, we learned how to make a bigger and stronger connection with each other, one that held space for this new stage of your life. Our lives had changed, but *Jesus* hadn't changed. He was the one holding us all together as we all grew. He is still holding us together.

I love you,
Mom

As our children grow, it can be tempting to try to hold them back for our own sake. When we do that, we actually hinder them and our relationship with them. Put all your weight on Jesus, and he will lead you and your child into those wider, greener spaces with more love for each other than you had before.

Dear Lord,

I have never walked through this season before, and I don't understand it. I pray that as my child and I are learning, we will be patient with each other. I pray for understanding and clarity, and that our bond would grow deeper in this season. Help us not to get frustrated with each other, but keep in mind that you have put us together and, therefore, you will give us the wisdom to communicate. I pray that we would listen more intently and love each other more deeply. May we allow space for each other to grow in this season at a new pace. May we acknowledge the growth that is happening in our relationship because we are seeking you for wisdom. I trust you, Lord.

In Jesus's name, Amen.

The Result of Grit

"In your majesty ride forth victoriously

in the cause of truth, humility and justice;

let your right hand achieve

awesome deeds."

Psalm 45:4

Dear Josh,

You've taught me so much about being a follower of God. I love looking back on your golf game. I can see how your focus on the golf course gradually shifted from your score to the people with you on the course. You had to face some high anxiety during your tournaments, but as you shifted your focus to others, your anxiety lessened. Son, your whole game changed. Your score didn't always get better, but your attitude about the round changed because you had often made a new friend on the golf course. You had so many amazing moments during those games, and I had so much fun encouraging you and feeding you so you could keep up your strength during the four hours of play. I watched you grow socially and become more extroverted, as other players would yell your name to say hello from all directions on the course. You had always dreamed of playing college golf, and you were working *so hard* to achieve your dream.

During your junior year, one of the worst things imaginable happened to our world and to you. COVID washed over the globe, and college recruiting was one of the many things that came to a halt. But even in the face of a pandemic, you continued to work hard, believing you would get an offer. We prayed for you and trusted you would get your chance. We were scared, but God began to open doors.

Remember the gentleman you invited to join you for a round of golf at a local course? He turned out to be friends with a coach you had been talking to. It was incredible to watch that man call the coach and put in a good personal word for you! Then, two weeks before recruiting season ended, you were able to meet with that coach. As you talked to him, he began to see your character and heart. You shared your scores and what you had learned during your golf season, but more importantly, you shared your vision to influence other players by encouraging them and being a good leader.

Praise God, a month later, he called you and offered you the golf scholarship we had been praying for all those years! We saw God's faithfulness to you unfold as you sought to follow him above all else. Your dad and I are so proud of you.

I love you,
Mom

Even when the odds seem insurmountable, God can "achieve awesome deeds" through and for our children. Encourage your child to focus not only on winning but also on having a mindset that values others. If they do this, they will win in all the ways that matter most.

Dear Jesus,

Thank you that it says in Jeremiah 29:11 that you, the God of the universe, have plans for my child. I believe your plan is good, and so I trust you with it. Sometimes I can't see past the daily grind, and during those times, I pray I would remember that I serve a God who is trustworthy. I know that you are able, and I believe that you are in control. I claim victory today, not by sight but by faith. Please help me Lord, to call on you all the days of my life. I need you.

In Jesus's name, Amen.

Trusting God's Plan

"Be strong and courageous. Do not be afraid or terrified because of them, for the LORD your God goes with you; he will never leave you nor forsake you."

Deuteronomy 31:6

Dear Lauren,

The day you came to your dad and me and said you didn't want to go to college, I felt so afraid for you. I had a plan for you, and it was for you *to get a four-year degree!* I honestly didn't know what to think when you explained that you wanted to explore getting a two-year ministry degree at Highlands College. I had prayed throughout your high school years that you would desire God more than anything, but when you said this was what you felt called to, I was at a loss! I felt the pull of the world and what it says the path of success looks like. I was afraid a ministry degree wouldn't prepare you for life. Looking back now, I see I was filled with fear.

All along, it was God who was calling you toward himself in a way that was unique to you, and it took such boldness and strength to choose it! Now look at what has come of the path you chose. You've grown into a beautiful young woman. You have an incredible job serving your local church. You've found the love of your life, Vidal. And now you have a precious baby of your own!

I'm so glad you followed God's plan, not mine, Lauren. He knew you even better than I did. You have always been a trendsetter. You go against the grain and follow your heart. In my fear, I thought you were going off the rails, but in reality, you were displaying courage, strength, and faith. You've helped me learn to be stronger and more courageous, too.

I love you,

Mom

When we teach our children to ask God for guidance, it shouldn't be a surprise when he gives it to them! Practice keeping an open mind and heart when your child has an idea that differs from yours. God won't forsake your child, and he won't forsake you.

Dear Lord,

I cannot see a clear path for my children. They have chosen a path that I did not expect. May I see your hand, hear their heart, and trust that you are their Wonderful Counselor. Your hands are bigger than mine, and I trust you to guide them. I don't have all the answers, but I pray that in these uncertain times I will trust you to attend to my children's needs. Please help me let go and let your hands hold them. I pray for wisdom beyond my years to shape my heart and allow me to hear your voice guiding me.

In Jesus's name, Amen.

The Gift of Showing Up

"Therefore, encourage one another and build each other up, just as in fact you are doing."

1 Thessalonians 5:11

Dear Katie,

Have you ever stopped to think about all the games and events you've attended over the years? Have you counted how many times you chose to support and encourage your brothers and sisters rather than making plans with your friends? I know turning down invitations from your friends was a sacrifice.

And you not only supported your siblings with your physical presence; you supported them emotionally. You offered solidarity and encouragement when their team lost or when they were disappointed in themselves. You experienced their heartache with them and understood when they were frustrated, angry, or sad. You always seemed to know how important it was for your siblings to see you in the stands cheering them on.

You have been such an encouragement to your dad, to me, and to your brothers and sisters, Katie. Your giving spirit has brought our family together in so many ways and created bonds between you and your siblings that have lasted into adulthood.

Thank you for being a living example of what encouragement looks like. Thank you for building us up.

I love you,

Mom

Empower your older children to use their influence for good in the lives of their little brothers or sisters. Remind them often of how important they are. Look for their gifts and notice how those gifts influence the family.

Dear Lord,

I pray that my children will understand the call you have placed on their lives to encourage the people you have chosen for them to walk with. Help them understand that you have handpicked our family. Teach them to encourage each other as no one else in the world can do. Friends may come and go, but they are together for life, and I pray that they would understand the importance of loving one another unconditionally. Thank you, Lord, that they all have a special way of communicating, and I pray they will see the need our family has for their unique voice.

In Jesus's name, Amen.

Formed by Faithful Men

"Listen my son to your father's instruction,

and do not forsake your mother's teaching.

They are a garland to grace your head

and a chain to adorn your neck."

Proverbs 1:8-9

Dear Josh, Jake, and Ryan,

There came a time, around age 13 or 14, when you needed to hear things from your father, a coach, or another man you respected, rather than from me. You were trying so hard to be grown-up, and hearing your mom tell you what to do didn't sit well with you. You were separating from me and growing into men. It was exactly what was supposed to happen, but I'll admit it hurt my feelings! I learned quickly that my role in your life was evolving. You were growing into young men yourselves and were better able to receive advice from a man. I would ask your father to tell you things or to talk with you when I saw you needed guidance. Sometimes after talking to you, he would tell me, "I don't know if they heard it or not." I know you did.

I watched you days, months, years later, taking that advice and integrating those changes into your life. This was one of the many ways your father and I learned to work together to help you grow. And I'm so proud of the men you've become.

I love you,

Mom

Whether a father lives in the home or not, it is so important for men to speak into our sons' lives. As boys differentiate from their mothers, they need men they can look up to and emulate. Male role models are not optional; they're essential!

Dear Lord,

May our sons understand the importance of having a male role model in their lives. May they desire to allow a man who is walking with you to pour wisdom and encouragement into their lives. I pray they would not be afraid to ask someone that you have put on their heart to be this type of godly mentor. Please counsel my son through this individual and allow him to grow in his knowledge of you. Sometimes it's hard to trust someone else to invest in my child, but I pray that you will give me peace. I know, from your Word, you say to seek wise counsel, so I pray this for my child. Most importantly, help them to seek your Word, understand your plan, and find peace in it.

In Jesus's name, Amen.

In It Together

"I appeal to you, brothers and sisters, in the name of our Lord Jesus Christ, that all of you agree with one another in what you say and that there be no divisions among you, but that you be perfectly united in mind and thought."

1 Corinthians 1:10

Dear Kids,

One of the things that stands out to me most as I look back over our years under the same roof—years that look far too short now that they're in our rearview mirror—is how grateful I am that you spent so much time together attending each other's games and events. You were there for each other in body and in spirit, cheering each other on, screens set aside, paying *attention*, together in the victories and the defeats.

It wasn't always easy for you to give up your plans for the weekend or the evening. Sometimes you had a lot of homework or missed another social event, but through the weeks, months, and years, you built something precious together. You built deep relationships with one another. Together, you built a place for everyone to belong. When one of you came home angry or sad because something didn't go as planned, the other kids didn't take it personally, because they were there with you at your event and understood why you were upset. You all helped each other work through frustration and disappointment. You were in it together.

I hope this is something you'll carry with you into your own families, along with the deep understanding that you're never alone. It took a lot of effort to make all those events happen, but we wouldn't trade one single minute spent together for the whole world now.

I love you,

Mom

It's worth every bit of effort it takes to get our children to their siblings' games, recitals, and events. It's an investment in their relationships and in the family as a whole. I promise that when they're grown up, you'll be so thankful for that time together!

Dear Lord,

Thank you for the sweet times that we've had together as a family. Some of these moments were difficult, but we thank you, Lord, that we experienced them together. I pray that our children will understand how important it is to stay connected all their lives. May the enemy never create a narrative in their minds that causes dissension among our children. I pray they would feel open to discuss what's inside their hearts and reach out to each other for help. Thank you that they love each other with reckless abandon; I know this is because you answered our prayer as parents. We prayed from the very beginning that our kids would get along well and would want to be together more than with anyone else in this world. Thank you, Lord, for answering our prayers.

Amen

Clarity Comes in the Quiet

"You will seek me and find me when you seek me with all your heart."

Jeremiah 29:13

Dear Kids,

I love you so much, and I just want to pour every bit of wisdom that I have into you. Part of me wants life to be easy, for you to always know what to do and how to do it. God hasn't made life that way, though. There will be many times when you're not sure what to do. Every day brings unique circumstances, and some of them will be difficult. I cannot tell you how important it is to persevere.

When you don't know what to do or which path to take, just keep taking the next step. You always have a choice about which perspective you will take, so stay hopeful. Know that wisdom will come to you. God will provide what you need when you need it, and you will figure it out!

Some days may be harder than others, but in the process of making it through those days, take time to be still. Sit in the quiet and trust that you will have clarity on whether to pursue an opportunity or not. Let your mind rest and think. It's very hard in this world of constant distraction and entertainment to be still, but please hear me: understanding comes *in the quiet.* I've learned this, and I am still working on this, and I hope you will learn it, too.

I love you,

Mom

If you need wisdom, take time to quiet your soul and seek God with all your heart. Ask him for direction, and trust that he'll provide it. When we learn how to practice this, we can teach our children to do the same.

Dear Lord,

Thank you that you say in your Word that we have the very mind of Christ. Lord, I pray our children would seek discernment from you to know how to speak and how to move. I pray that you would give them a heart that hungers after you, so they will know how to help those around them. May our children have confidence in you when they speak to others of your forgiveness and love. May they have understanding beyond their years.

In Jesus's name, Amen.

God's Provision in Every Moment

"As for God, his way is perfect:

the LORD's word is flawless; he shields

all who take refuge in him."

2 Samuel 22:31

Dear Kids,

There are many moments in our lives when we don't think anyone sees us or notices us. I want you to know that God sees and knows everything that concerns you.

Once Ryan forgot his tennis rackets at school, and for the life of me, I could not figure out how we were going to get his rackets, eat lunch, and get to his tennis tournament on time! I scrambled for about ten minutes, trying to figure out what to do. I couldn't see a way forward. Then God put it in your dad's mind to call us and ask if he could do anything for us! He had planned to work at a coffee shop before meeting up with us, but he had a strong feeling that he was supposed to call us instead. As soon as his call came through, I realized that *God knew the trouble we were in,* and he used your dad to give us the help we needed! (And how wonderful is your father?!)

It's amazing how God is in the details of our lives. He knows exactly what we need and how to help us. We are not perfect, but God is perfect, and he loves us with his whole heart. You can always put your weight down on that.

I love you,

Mom

Through the years, I've learned that God knows and sees everything that concerns us. Practice noticing how God provides what you and your family need, and point them out to your children. Soon they'll learn to see those things for themselves.

Dear Lord,

Thank you for being in the details of every moment of our lives. I pray that we would see you moving among our children and that they would recognize your presence. Help me to teach our children that you care about the very small things that concern them. Help them to understand that your heart is *for* them and not *against* them. I pray the love you have for them will fill them with confidence and courage to face anything that comes their way. You are in the moments, and we hope in your Word.

In Jesus's name, Amen.

Big Emotions, Bigger God

"Better a patient person than a warrior, one with self-control than one who takes a city."

Proverbs 16:32

Dear Kids,

Sometimes being a mom is so hard! I feel frustrated and struggle to hold my tongue. I want to do the talking, and I want *you* to just be quiet and listen! I'm grateful for God's patience when he sees me doing the very things I'm trying to help you learn *not* to do. I often think that because I can see the bigger picture, you should, too. I'm sorry for all the times I put myself at the center of things and just couldn't get it together. I know my emotional temperature affected everyone in the house.

It's true for all of us. Our attitudes and emotions affect everyone around us. Over the years, I learned that when you had huge emotions welling up inside of you, telling someone how you were feeling helped so much! You would feel seen and cared for and could be encouraged, and everyone else could be spared from fearing they had done something to cause your explosion!

When I lost my patience or said something I regretted, I learned repeatedly how much I needed the Lord's help. I had to lean on his grace to get me through the "ugly times" of my day. We all must practice self-control, and we need Jesus and each other to do it. It's beautiful to learn humility and to learn how to depend on the Lord for patience and strength. I'm glad we were able to learn that together.

I love you,

Mom

When you notice big emotions welling up, pause, pray, and tell someone else! If you model this and teach this to your children, it will help them learn to reach out to those who love them for support. These are skills that will serve them well their whole lives.

Dear Lord,

Forgive me for having an attitude when I don't get my way. When I expect one of our children to act a certain way and they don't, I pray that I would teach from a place of grace. I pray that I would remember how many times you have probably looked at me and were disappointed in the way I acted. Help me to be a better listener and to speak more slowly. I come to you now asking for discernment, patience, and encouragement. Give me a listening spirit and a lot of grace. I want to know, Lord, how to instruct my children for your glory. Please Lord, guide me when I am weary, and please give me strength.

In Jesus's name, Amen.

Led By God Not Others

"Hold on to instruction, do not let it go;

guard it well, for it is your life."

Proverbs 4:13

Dear Kids,

I know sometimes you were frustrated by how our family had different rules from other families. When you're growing up, it's hard not to feel that your own family's rules are unfair sometimes. I hope you can look back now and see more of our reasons for why we limited games, screens, phones, movies, and so forth. Your dad and I just wanted to make sure you had space to grow in healthy ways, and we knew we were responsible for providing that.

When you questioned our rules, I remember saying things like, "You know what? I have a conviction about this. I've prayed about it, and I believe this is right for our family." Dad and I leaned in and owned those boundaries, and I think it made you feel safe to know we were watching out for you (even if you weren't always happy about it).

We were also setting an example for you to follow with your own friends when you felt pressured to do something you weren't comfortable with. We wanted you to be able to say, "That may be good for you, but it's not good for me." We wanted to give you language to use and to help you get comfortable standing apart from the crowd.

We asked ourselves, "Who are the Brelands? What do *we* do? What do *we* value?" We wanted our home to be a house of prayer. We wanted to stand on the foundation of who God is. I would tell you, "I don't have all the answers, but I'm seeking God, and I answer to him. I'm accountable to him for the decision I make on your behalf, and this is what I understand that he is telling me is right for *our* family."

I watch each of you now and see how you have learned to stand for what's right in your own lives. Dad and I are so very proud of you.

I love you,
Mom

Ask God for wisdom about what your family rules should be, then own those decisions. Don't be afraid to stand firm in your convictions, and you will teach your children to do the same.

Dear Lord,

Please help my children not to compare our family with any other family. I pray that our children understand how intently we pray for your will to be accomplished in the heart of our family. It's hard to swim upstream and be bold. I pray, Father, that we would care more about what you think than what our children or anyone else thinks about our actions. We want to please you. When we are weary, please give us courage to stay strong and not to compromise. We promise to pray without ceasing so that we can make wise decisions on behalf of our family. We commit our family back to you.

In Jesus's name, Amen.

From Our Home to Yours:

Ten Timeless Traditions to

Nurture Faith and Family

Traditions have been such a meaningful part of our family's life. They help create a home with predictable rhythms where kids have fun-filled events to look forward to, and they also create a deep sense of security and belonging. Some of our family's traditions are just for Jeremy and me, while others include our big extended family. Big or small, each one has become deeply meaningful to us. Traditions have a way of becoming sacred, like liturgy, filling the years with a joyful cadence that's unique to your family. I hope our traditions inspire you to create your own family customs that bring a holy rhythm to your family's days, weeks, and years.

Morning Devotionals

One of my very favorite times of day is my morning devotional with Jeremy. Every day we set our alarms for 6:00 a.m., wake up, get our coffee, and then get back into bed with our Bibles and journals. Sometimes we sit in the quiet, other times, we have instrumental worship music playing softly in the background. This is such a comforting time of day, where we can be still before the Lord and let his love soak into our spirits. We'll spend some time journaling, asking the Lord, "What do you have for me right now?" Then we'll come back together and share Scriptures or insights the Lord gave us individually. Finally, we'll tell each other about the events we have coming up that day, and we'll pray for each other.

I truly believe this is the practice that has kept our marriage so strong through the years and has made us better parents. Because we stay connected and united before the Lord, we stay open to each other. Throughout the day, we can check in on each other and let each other know we're praying for that meeting, doctor's appointment, or whatever it may be. And it's been such an encouragement to watch each other grow in faith over the years. There's no way to overstate what a gift this practice has been in our marriage and our family.

Scripture Memorization

When Jeremy and I started dating, we started memorizing Scripture together. We knew we needed God's Word to sustain us in the busyness of college, and as you know, life only gets busier from there! The practice was so important to us that we continued it with our children. Every night, usually at bedtime, we would spend a few minutes together as a family practicing a passage of Scripture. We would say a few words at a time, and the next night we would add a few more words. Pretty soon, we would have the whole verse or passage memorized.

As the kids grew, they carried these Scriptures with them to school, the dance studio, the soccer field, the golf course, and more. Whenever they felt off-balance or anxious, I would remind them, "Say your verses." By meditating on these promises from God from the time they were little, our children learned to trust God's Word more than any fear that rose up against them.

As you're learning to memorize the Bible with your children, ask God to give you a special verse for your family. Our family verse is Zephaniah 3:17: "The Lord your God is with you, the Mighty Warrior who saves. He takes great delight in you; he quiets you with his love and rejoices over you with singing." Holding fast to a verse of Scripture as a family tells your kids: "This is what is written, and this is what we believe. God is going to sing over us." Ask God to give your children a life verse, and when life feels uncertain, they can return to it repeatedly!

Food Wars

"Food Wars" was something we did to make dinner time more fun, and the kids thought it was a blast! Our family loved to watch a food competition show together, and it inspired us to create our own cooking competition. We'd divide into teams, and the assignment might be to make a dessert or an appetizer, or another dish for the meal. Sometimes I'd give the kids a list of limited ingredients, and they had to cook using only those few items. The results were so funny!

When the food was ready, I'd ask a neighbor or my parents to judge the competition and choose a winner, then we'd all enjoy all the food together. We had so much fun and laughed so hard! Ryan created this drink called "Clemon Lemon." It's lemonade, fresh-squeezed clementine juice, and sugar. Everyone still loves it to this day!

The kids learn a lot through this activity. They learn to work together. They learn to use their voice to advocate for what they want to make. They learn to cook and what they like to cook. I think it also made our kids appreciate me more as the cook in the family, because they saw how much time and work went into preparing food. Give it a try with your family and see what you think!

High/Low/Go

Dinner time is such an integral part of family life, and the conversation and time together are just as important as the food. I used this question to get our family's conversation started every night before dinner: "What was today's high, low, and go?" That's just a quick way of asking, what was the best part of your day, the worst part of your day, and something you learned today that you can take action on? To answer the go question, for example, someone might say that they learned a new way to be a better friend or that they could have studied more for a test they took that day. This conversation starter almost always opened up the door to deeper discussions, and it gave Jeremy and me the chance to take a deeper dive into the kids' days. Almost always, after answering these questions, the kids would just start talking. I even use this sometimes to help a child get started when he or she was sharing a big experience—like a mission trip, for example. It's just a great way to get a conversation going. See if it works at your dinner table!

Talk Time

Talk time was a nightly bedtime tradition that we implemented when the kids were younger. Since our kids shared rooms, they always wanted to stay up late and talk! Jeremy and I put that desire to good use. This practice is so simple; if you have young children, you can start tonight.

Let the kids know they're going to get a new bedtime privilege called "Talk Time," which will allow them to stay up a little later. (We made our time anywhere from three to ten minutes.) Depending on their attitude that day and the time we were actually getting them tucked in, we would give them a few extra minutes of "Talk Time" to catch up with each other. Once they're all tucked in, you might set a timer so they can see how many minutes they have left. This practice made bedtime more fun and gave them an incentive to get their pajamas on and complete their nighttime routines.

Sometimes, if they had been working extra hard or we had a little wiggle room in our timeline, Jeremy and I would show up with a plate of snacks and say, "Just kidding! We're all going to have 'Talk Time'!" and they thought that was the absolute most fun. This little practice worked on many levels, and it encouraged them to build deeper relationships with each other, which was what we wanted most of all.

Lunch with Dad

When the kids were really young, I took them to have lunch with Jeremy every week. It was an amazing time, not just for the kids but for me, too! I would load the kids into the car, and we would head off to Dad's office. Sometimes we took our lunches, and sometimes we picked up lunch on the way. If the weather was nice, we might eat at a picnic table outside, or we might eat inside at the cafeteria. The kids loved seeing where Jeremy worked, and I loved getting out of the house for a little while! The kids also enjoyed going into Dad's office and saying hello to his colleagues. They might sit in his chair and pretend to work or enjoy a piece of special candy that he had at his office. These weekly outings also provided a wonderful learning opportunity. As the kids and I prepared for the visit, we would talk about the importance of good manners, such as speaking in an "office voice" or saying hello and shaking hands. We all looked forward to that time together every week, and now that the kids are grown, I have so many sweet memories of those lunches together.

Date Nights with the Kids

In a big family, one-on-one time with each child is so precious. To make sure we had this quality time with each child built into our lives, Jeremy and I made a point to take our kids on date nights. For some reason, time at a restaurant or ice cream shop, away from the distractions of home, would open the door to deep conversations that helped us get to know our children so much better.

Sometimes we did group dates where Jeremy would take the boys to do something fun, like go-carting, and I would take the girls out for pedicures or something we enjoyed. Dates with your kids can look a thousand different ways, and they don't have to be expensive. The important thing is to have fun and to intentionally create space for deeper conversation and connection. Try it and see if you have as much fun as we did!

Valentine's Day Scavenger Hunt

Our family's longest-running tradition is the annual Valentine's Day Scavenger Hunt. We've been creating these hunts for more than twenty years, and the kids love it! Here's how it works.

First, choose a special location for the hunt. Select a place with plenty of shops or interesting spots where you can hide the gifts. We always do our scavenger hunt in the downtown area of our hometown, Franklin, Tennessee. Next, choose five specific locations where you'll hide the gifts, then create five large paper hearts in different colors. Write a clue for each location on each of the five hearts. I usually print out our clues, but you can also write them by hand. Once the clues are complete, stack the hearts, punch a hole in the left top corner of the stack, and tie them all together with a ribbon. This stack of hearts will be what you will give your kids. Every clue leads to a location, and each location holds a little gift, like a small bag of candy or a toy. (You'll need to hide the prizes before the scavenger hunt begins.) We try to make our clues funny or silly, like an inside joke or a memory from a past family experience. You could make them rhyme if you're ambitious. The last clue leads to the final location and the biggest prize. One year, I hid a gift containing a swimsuit for each child and the announcement of a family beach trip! Your last prize doesn't have to be that big, though. You could make the last stop an ice cream shop, and the prize is an ice cream cone for everyone. Just make it something that your family would enjoy.

Jeremy and I always laugh so hard when we're coming up with the clues, so creating the hunt is something fun for us to do as a couple. The kids have so much fun and practice working together as a team without even realizing they're doing it. And the one who figures out the clue always *always* feels so special! This activity also strengthens family bonds because the clues often evoke family memories, and we all enjoy reminiscing about sweet times we've shared as a family. There are so many benefits to this tradition, but the biggest one is just having fun together!

Birthday Celebrations

Birthdays are a big deal in our house. Since we have a large family, major holidays come with time and financial restraints, and the kids must share with their siblings year-round.

Birthdays are the time when we can really focus on one child and show him or her how special he or she is to us.

The night before a child's birthday, Jeremy and I decorate the house together. We use a traditional birthday banner that we hang in the same place every year (I personalize it with the birthday child's photo and name). We have pre-packaged birthday decorations (streamers, garlands, paper lanterns, pom poms, and so forth) that we reuse for all the birthdays. In addition to the standard decorations, we use items unique to the birthday boy or girl. For example, Josh was our golfer, so on his birthday, I might gather his golf gear and incorporate it into the decorations. I might write encouraging notes and put them on his golf clubs. When the kids were little, they loved these little stuffed animals called Webkins, so I would gather all the Webkins in the house and line the stairs with them. Be as creative as you want!

On the birthday night, we'd serve that child's favorite foods for dinner, and afterward, we would have the Birthday Blessing. For the Birthday Blessing, the child of honor gets to choose whether he or she wants everyone to say one word, one sentence, or ask a question. Then everyone follows that formula and shares what they love about that child or asks a question that lets everyone get to know that child better. It's a precious time every year, and the birthday child feels so encouraged and loved.

After the birthday blessing, we all pray over that child for the coming year. Finally, we end the evening with the birthday child's favorite treat. It could be cake or chips and queso—whatever he or she would like!

On special birthdays, it could be 10, 13, 16, 18, we sometimes planned a small trip with that child or did something extra exciting. It could be anything from a day hiking to a trip to New York City, depending on your time and money budget. But all the kids agree, the affirmation and blessing time is always what meant the most to them, and that didn't cost a penny!

Christmas Celebrations

We start celebrating Christmas at the beginning of December. We trim our tree and display all the Christmas decorations, of course. We also try to find a special Christmas concert that we can all dress up for and attend as a family, something really special. We usually set aside a shopping day when we all go to the mall and do our last-minute shopping together. Christmas Eve day is always for stocking stuffer shopping! We collect small items like socks, candy, or small toys (and always a giant peppermint stick) for each stocking.

We often make family Christmas cards on Christmas Eve, too, and we always attend our church's Christmas Eve service. Sometimes we go out to dinner before the service and sometimes after. There was a stretch of years when we made steak and shrimp for dinner and ate around the coffee table in the living room with candles. After dinner, we'd tell each other how we'd seen each other growing throughout the year, and we'd share how we experienced God that year.

On Christmas Day, we usually read the Christmas story, then open our presents and have a special brunch of egg-and-cheese croissants, monkey bread, and fruit parfaits. We always invite our extended family over for brunch, just talk and share about what we'd like to see God do in the years ahead. For Christmas dinner, we usually have turkey, mashed potatoes, and green beans, and a Happy Birthday cake for Jesus.

We believe it's important for our kids to get gifts for each other, so we encourage that. For our extended family, we set a budget and draw names. And while we must be mindful of money during the holidays, we want to show the children how important it is to share what we have with others. Each year, we find a family we can serve and buy gifts for, and when we go out for our Christmas meal, we love to leave the server an enormous tip! It feels amazing to bless others this way and the children learn that Jesus's words were true; it actually is more wonderful to give than to receive.

Homemade Christmas Cards

My dad started this card-making tradition, and our kids absolutely love it. You can make this event as big or as small as you want. In our family, we get together with my parents and my siblings' families, but a small, intimate gathering would be just as special in its own way.

First, set aside a block of time on your family calendar for card-making, so everyone saves the date. When the time comes, if you have several people participating, everyone can work together to set up so all the work doesn't land on you! Ask one person to put on Christmas music, another to make hot chocolate or distribute the card supplies, and so forth. (I have a card-making drawer in our home that is always filled with card stock, fun markers, and lots of stickers!)

Once everything is set up, gather around the table and start creating! When our family was smaller, we each made cards for every single person in our family. Now that our extended family has grown so large, we make a card for each family rather than everyone. When we get together for Christmas, we exchange cards, and the recipient reads them to the family. We try to follow my dad's lead and incorporate humor into them, so it's always funny to hear them read aloud!

The kids learn so many things from this practice: to be creative, to develop skillfulness with words, and to see how their efforts make others feel loved and encouraged, just to name a few. I hope you'll try this and that it will bring just as much joy to your family as it has to ours!

In conclusion, I wanted to thank you for walking this journey with me. It has been amazing to think back over the last thirty-one years and ponder God's faithfulness. I pray that God will guide your family over the years into a deeper relationship with him and each other. I pray that you will have clarity and momentum every day. It's not easy, but with God's help it is possible. It has been so rewarding and looking back I would not trade one day for anything. In this season, pray continually for God to guide you and press into the lessons you learn along the way. A family has a lot of lessons to teach one another. I pray for patience, diligence, discernment and love to flow in and out of you from this day forth.

www.ingramcontent.com/pod-product-compliance
Lightning Source LLC
Chambersburg PA
CBHW032056120726
48054CB00002B/6
* 9 7 9 8 9 9 5 2 0 5 4 0 1 *